THINKING EGG

Thinking Egg
JACQUELINE BROWN

LITTLEWOOD ARC

Published by Littlewood Arc
Nanholme Mill, Shaw Wood Road
Todmorden, Lancs. OL14 6DA.

Copyright © 1993 Jacqueline Brown
Copyright © 1993 Littlewood Arc

Design by Tony Ward
Printed by Arc & Throstle Press Ltd.
Nanholme Mill, Todmorden, Lancs.
Typeset by Anne Lister Typesetting
Brunswick House, South Street, Halifax.

ISBN 0 946407 89 4

Thinking Egg – The Sequence was awarded first prize in the Arvon/Observer International Poetry Competition 1992.

The publishers acknowledge financial assistance from Yorkshire and Humberside
Arts Board, North West Arts Board and
East Midlands Arts.

Extracts from Delia Smith's Cookery Course Parts 1 and 2 are reproduced with the permission of BBC Enterprises Limited.

CONTENTS

Particular / 9
Baby Egg / 11
In the Room I / 12
Egg-Gathering with Lily / 13
Pubertal Egg / 14
Naming of Cuckoo / 15
Yesterday When I Was Young / 17
Egg Woman at Her Wedding / 19
Coq au vin / 20
In the Room II / 22
Fairy Tale / 24
Poaching / 25
Seismic / 26
In the Room III / 28
Scrambled / 30
Analytic Egg I / 31
Analytic Egg II / 32
Finality of Egg / 33
Theatre / 34
Cuckoo Calling / 36
At the Garden Centre / 37
Separating Eggs / 38
Gifts / 39
Lemon Soufflé Omelette / 40
Thinking Egg / 41
About the author / 43

Lady, the sunlit hour is beautiful
And beautiful when wind blows soft the sea
And earth in her spring flower and affluent streams.
Of many beauties I could tell the praise
But none there is beams on the eye so bright
As when the childless, heartsore with desire,
See children like young buds about their house.

      Euripides

Involuntary childlessness affects an estimated 15% of couples in the U.K.

      N.A.C.

Eggs are full of life containing nutrients, proteins, fats, vitamins, minerals and a tiny pocket of air – nearly everything essential for living.

    Delia Smith's Cookery Course, Part 1.

Particular

Palm size, shaped to hand,
so light a burden
cold from the kitchen
rough gritskin puckering thumbtip,
iridescent smear of stuck straw
a skid of farmyard muck or henshit.

Baby Egg

Last egg, offering nearly everything
essential to life in a baby's hand.
First baby, topheavy bandy but willing
to lurch from Auntie to Mother, bearing
the last egg of the ration. Mother's memory
of egg.   Not mine.
A tale plucked from the scarce heap of story
retained to niggle questions. What
possessed them? What mischief governed
such a gamble with only egg? Oooh-ooh
the lifted breath as one foot rears
tremors   finds earth   Aaaaah   as
hand swivels   stays   rights itself.
That's right.   Clever baby.   Bring the egg.
What was in the four blue eyes?
Not my memory. A blank.
Eyes of the sisters are ash now. Egg
in my hand to break and cook and eat.
The palm contracts.
Crushed egg slimes between joints and knuckles,
cauls the boat of the hand like sperm or snot.

In the Room I

Come too late to see
the eyes someone's
thumbed shut.
Anger like shutters
slamming,
pity slicking the throat,
the nasal membrane swells,
oozes; tears are furious
hot.
Not for her. She's gone.
This one's for me.
That dreadful shift of face
from quick to this,
to dirty tallow,
yolk-eyes filmed over
by solid cataracts of skin,
these cheeks landslipped
from nose, no lips,
under the tautened sheet
how flat, how shrunk –
blown shell, husk.
Windows shut. Curtains still.
Is it temper that so stirs air?
Does air move of itself?
Or is it longing that rucks
the bedclothes
that lets the sigh go out?

A nurse says, ashes and urns and years later . . . *it's just sometimes the newly-dead don't lie still, seem to live for a moment, move slightly, sigh or fart as a tiny pocket of air escapes.*

Egg-Gathering with Lily

Nan, fat as the butter she spreads so lavish
melting the toast to yellow finger-smears.
Holiday Nan, uncorseted and featherbed muzzy,
slurring her slippers from table to stove
black pan atilt in her hand, egg an island
in limpid fat, edges all wave-bitten lace.
Godda feed you up a bit. Skinny Min.
Get you strong. Eat up. Good girl.
Egg's good for you. Eggs is meat.

Warrior Nan in her pinny with her zinc bucket
shield that swings and chimes the time it takes
to walk between backstep and henhouse, the last
fat forkful and the fright of feathers.
Skinny Min unwilling to fight the weight of hen,
eyes shut tight against beakstab and flutter,
throat closed down on the pressure of hot egg
on palm. *That's right. Clever girl. Careful.*
Put the egg in the bucket.

Pubertal Egg

Skinny Min hovering at the women's margins.
They are shelling peas, telling stories.
Min is not listening but she can't not hear
the secret voices with their *birth blood death*
she can't not see their solid hands
that split the pods so neat apart, fingers
so strong hooking the green spheres
in one continuous rain to rattle in the pan.

She thieves one: it is cool and thin in her palm
like a finger. Hers are too flimsy, clumsy,
to force the split and gape as the women do.
Her pod rips to ragged holes – she must peel
off skin to find green beads in satiny beds.
She does not want to tear tiny slivers of cord
that hold them safe. Careful, she unpicks one;
pads of first finger and thumb gentle it.

Soon she must speak of that irregular stain
on the sheet on the bed in the bedroom above,
its red curling to biscuit to brown – etching
a miniature antique map of a continent. Soon.
But not now. Now she raises finger and thumb,
the green seed solid between them. She drops it
onto her tongue, closes her lips, swallows hard,
then smiles. One pea cannot fatten her.

Naming of Cuckoo

Outside it's beginning to be almost spring
    inside girl in a gymslip, a blouse,
    a bodice, a vest, brown flannel
    knickers, ankle socks, laceup shoes;
    girl at a desk

invisibly trees heave up their tons of water

    girl in a classroom listening and
    learning the habits of Cuckoo while
    brown flannel rusts orange absorbing
    her failed egg

leaves on the flooding trees are only potential

    girl writes in an orange-backed notebook
    Cuculinae – underlined – *Migration*
    – underlined, altered: *Migratory*
    Route

windows sting as May alters; becomes April; alters

    arrows track her traced map – bird
    prints northward from Africa, north
    to Europe to here where she's learning
    Cuculinae build no nests

near-spring leans on the windows, wanting in

    teacher's breasts are cradled eggs
    in nylon cups , vest, nylon slip
    and blouse... teacher dictates :-
    parasitic.. polymorphic.. mimetic *eggs*

Outside something not-quite mimes authentic
                                            spring

girl understands: she is a good girl,
a clever girl and her secret eggs are hidden,
safe as houses against predation –
nor springs nor cuckoos can frighten her.

Yesterday When I Was Young

The morning after *La Ronde* at the Cine
on the Boulevard de Batignolles
he is feeding me soft-boiled egg
from a tarnished spoon. His eyes are freckle
brown, my lips are light pink and open
like a chick's and his are open too, sympathetic.

Look how artfully while he was busy
boiling I've draped the grey sheet.
Look how languidly while he's feeding me
egg I stroke his sculpted lip with one
pink finger, not smiling, trying for
the authentic smoulder.

Charles Aznavour on the turntable caresses
the air, his syllables so controlled and quick
like tongue-flicks all over my bare shoulders,
my artful, part-covered breasts – *Hier encore
j'avais vingt ans, je caressais le temps,
j'ai joué de la vie...*

Were he to open them the French windows
would open inwards, the beige books discover
fat ragged pages that I understand. *Le Monde*
lies wrecked on the floor, his door has a foreign
locking system that I comprehend. I can stand
the foreign consistency of his *oeufs mollets*

and Aznavour's tremolo is doing unmentionable
things to my sheet covered crevices, my lips
are crinkling, and frightened tutting Mother
with her talk of darkened doorsteps and ignorance
of what the world is coming to is miles and
a stretch of sea and miles away

and *hier encore j'avais vingt ans* but today
I'm Jeanne Moreau and Catherine Deneuve and Bardot
all rolled into one and it's 17th of January 1964
and I'm twenty-one and in Paris and I've found
the authentic *vie* ...Oh, I love myself so much
at this moment, I could eat me.

Note: *hier encore j'avais vingt ans* – only yesterday I was twenty
oeufs mollets – soft boiled eggs

Egg Woman at Her Wedding

She comes in a range of colours
from milkwhite through bisque
and biscuit to a warm honey brown
though her contents are identical.
Her size may vary though the categories
are arbitrary – small, medium, standard,
large, numbered one to seven.
She is always symmetrical, always smooth,
always perfect for holding in the cup
of a hand.
At this moment she is white medium, size 4.
She has been candled for quality – the light
has detected no crack or blemish.

Someone has drawn a face on her –
two circles for eyes, two pinprick dots
for nose, a widened U for a mouth.
This face is innocent and complacent.
She looks almost sly.
She is so sure of her perfection.

She cannot know it cannot last.
When she is held safe in the handcup
she cannot foresee the moment
she will be cracked and eaten,
or the worse moment when somebody
– this boy, maybe, or a robber man –
will prick her either end
with a fine needle and blow her goodness
till her smooth fine features
will hide nothing. Unless a tiny pocket
of air can be called something.

*A truly authentic Coq au vin is made, obviously, with
a cock-bird and some of the blood goes into the sauce,
which, by the time it reaches the table, is a rich,
almost black colour.*
      Delia Smith's Cookery Course Part 2

Coq au vin

The flat is painted white as a cell
white as the inside of a shell

the marks are tentative yet – preliminary ..
they're learning something of all that's essential
for living together; how to sidestep slightly
to avoid collision and cracking, how to come close
without cracking in the hot bed –

the bed grows wider, larger, till there's room for more
and more: sometimes the empty margins oppress.. but
nothing so simple as to people them   There's M and A
and C and N and B and J – *we'll entertain – we'll stun
them with French cuisine*

so down to the market... she didn't know he loves markets,
his voice rises – she hears   fresh   raw   exciting
at the meat stall *he* does the talking (not mentioning
cocks of course for the butcher is loud and lewd
and over the slant belly his apron's stiff with blood).

plucked and sagging boiling-fowl hang long and flat,
off white like overused lard, like a morning face
stippled blue with small sharp shards of barb,
heads, legs, claws lolling, still coloured in
like the start of a painting

can't not look as butcher cleavers them off, tosses them
to an invisible bin... butcher's hair is slick and black
like *his* dead Dad's... butcher's fingers are thick and white:
butcher narrows eyes at her past *his* eyes .. winks
That's right, chuck,   long and slow,   lo o ong and slow

the white kitchen, the body slumped on the formica
You must do it..... but she can't not watch his hand,
his wrist deep in the flesh, then slurping out guts
and hundreds, thousands of tiny red eggs, potential
eggs – not laughing, his hair as black as his Dad's

far too young for the truly authentic, two of them
retching into the sink, binning the corpse,
drinking the burgundy, ringing the takeaway . .
their bile becomes one bile sliming the plug, and the plughole
two pairs of eyes squint right past each other into dark.

In the Room II

On blue paper sheeting
a woman is lying
on her side, knees to nose
like an ovenready chicken

another woman is stroking
her hand clenched till skin
feels close to tearing, like
she's a baby like she's a child

Just relax if you can
Clever girl   that's right

a man in a clean white coat's
an invisible voice moving
unseen in the greenpaint room
just a paper rustle, a mumble

she is not a clever girl
she is not a good girl
the snap of the rubber glove
condemns; the blue paper rucks
with her guilt

under a rubber membrane fingers
inquire, tamper – slick fingers
with no face eyes colour hair –
she has unbodied his fingers

Try to relax   it'll hurt less

a woman is severing a body into bits
guillotine snaps and the head floats
free, snap and snap through the pubic
bone and the body rises, next the legs;
on the blue paper sheet is a tiny pocket
of air encased in stoneskin and a wet
finger learning something   and a mind
recording   determined to forget

the other woman is helping her from the bed
saying *It's all right, it's all over,*
saying *There, dear* ... but the silly eyes
can't not look at the map of Africa
damp-etched on the blue paper sheeting
can't not fast forward to all the miles
and miles to go .. desert and sea
and desert and sea before the ghost
of a landing

Fairy Tale

There are trees. She slinks
among them with an empty belly.
There is a house that is bursting
with kids. The kids' mother
has gone off shopping. She is a bad mother,
leaving her kids thus. She would
not miss a kid. One soft milky
kid less would mean nothing to her.

A story mothers read to children
before sleeping, starting *Once
upon a time*, starting like memory
at no-date, no-place, no-time.

There is a door. She knocks on the door
raprap, pleading for, wanting in.
But the kids are good kids.
The kids are wise in the ways of tales.
They demand to see her fingers.
Dipped in flour, her fingers are white
as a mother's, white as a nanny's.

You can imagine it from their point of view –
the sneck lifted, the flurry, the panicky cries,
their sharp hooves' scatter . . .
a memory they'll consign to blankness,
to the hot dark they can only grope after.

Look how her belly has swollen now.
Look at the silly content smile as she sleeps.
Imagine her point of view when she wakens
in the black of the well-shaft, the pinpoint sky
that could be a million miles away
and her belly packed to bursting with stones.

Poaching

You could assemble a whole catalogue of 'do's and don'ts' on the subject of poaching eggs . . . . Don't attempt to poach more than two unless you're a really experienced hand.
                    Delia Smith's Cookery Course Part 1.

She has heard the women whispering
in hospital rooms of suffering,
pain, blood.

She has stood palefaced in the margins
looking and listening, separate
from them.

While they slept, she has walked in her head
through the bluelit quiet ward, skirting
the nurse,

toe-stepped along the white corridor,
keeping to walls, to where milky kids
snuffle;

she's walked further to a flurried place
where infants lie flat under glass, taped
to tubes.

Sleepwalking, she has understood theft,
the urge to prise open, steal and hide,
not care

that another woman is crying somewhere
just so long as her own boat of arms
is full.

Seismic

The bed is new and hard as a floor;
the sheet's new cotton, starched stiff.

This is the life! The man is lying
flat on his back with closed eyes.

She won't, can't, doesn't answer – too hot,
too hot and too hard to roll over and open –

the gap between is because margins are cooler.
Wait and sometime soon they'll sleep.

*

while they lie sleeping
room corners are shifting
light fixtures shivering
invisible things colliding
under the marble bedroom floor
under the shell of rock and earth

*

Nought point four on the Richter Scale –
minimum damage – their house not altered a jot:

older houses, Panaiottis tells them, have pillars
distorted, rooves caved in and buckled floors.

Kosta lala's to Mouskouri on the taverna jukebox
Enas mythos tha sas po, pou ton mathame paedia

Kosta is newly married; Kosta is BSc. Manchester;
except for muddled tenses his English is idiomatic.

My wife, they hear, *are in bed when it happens;
my wife tells me   for her the earth   moved.*

His mouth, laughing, is a dark hole they can't not
stare into. Two pairs of eyes stare into it.

Nothing needs saying – they've seen the ruins of Sparta.
Something has changed. A story's over. Ever-afters start here.

Note: *Enas mythos tha sas po, pou ton mathame paedia*
    I'll tell you a story I learned as a child

In the Room III

In the dayroom the woman is sitting,
back to the TV, watching the wall.
The woman's body is rocking
forward back, forward back,
ticktock ticktock.
Fragments of song
dribble from her mouth.
If anyone were listening
they'd hear *chicken egg baby* then
half-audible runs of wordless tune.

No-one is listening.

If the woman were to turn
anyone watching would see
how each cupped palm cradles an elbow
holds it still against the body's motion.
Anyone looking would see a stone oval
where the face should be, two blobs
of blue glass at its widest point.

No-one is looking.

If Stoneface were to rotate
from yellow wall to direct light
the blue glass blobs would see spring
framed in the window – a green lawn
spattered with dandelions,
a horsechestnut bursting,
a sky brailled with birds.

She will not turn.

If anyone were recording the scene
nothing would happen –
back-view of a to-fro rocking woman,
tiny clutches of song
pan-out to yellow walls
a yolk-spattered lawn
pan-in to a black and white TV.

No-one is recording,

No-one has the technology
to record the clackclack
of a mind speedshuttling
woof across frayed warp
weaving what may turn out to be
a cradle-cloth or winding sheet,

no-one knows.

Scrambled

it's dark   don't like the dark
sing a song make the dark go away
look what they've done to my song, Ma
lalalalalalala must've done wrong
bad egg   cracked egg   smacksmacksmack
poor egg   poor hen   Humpty Dumpty Dad
in bits and pieces all the King's horses
and all the King's men can't put Humpty
together again   "puir wee hen" says Humpty
when baby stumbles and tumbles   when the bough
breaks   puir wee hen when when when will you lay
me an egg for my tea? Not a stone egg   Silly
hen   Bad hen   smacksmack   sticks and stones
will break my bones   chop off her head.
The blood's all red
look what they've done to my brain, Ma
they've picked it like a chicken-bone
and chickchickchickchick chicken Run quick
cradle's falling Ma   catch Baby Bunting
fetch Daddy   Daddy's gone a hunting somebody
catch her too late can't put her together
again   say something
Bye Baby Bunting   bye baby   baby doesn't
like the dark   sing song make dark go away

Analytic Egg I

Cold room. A woman's voice is telling stories,
tales whose essential truths she's clutching for.
This tale is about Easter in another country –
people who crack red eggs saying χριστοσ ανεστγ!
saying He is risen indeed!

And yet in here – the man's voice is disembodied,
low, issuing from behind her back – *In here, you
refuse this resurrection.* Hate slimes her palms.
She'll smear his telltruth mouth shut with albumen.
Don't speak again. Hug your stories close, safe,
till the hour ends.

Nights, she dreams he is her lover. His penis
is pure white and erect as a pointed finger.
She bears his child, that sits on her immaculate lap,
the two of them hieratic in a yellow gold ellipse
like an icon.

Note: χριστοσ ανεστγ Christ is risen

Analytic Egg II

grasped words are just instruments –
scalpels surgical scissors cotton swabs –
tools to help dissect the mind

sometimes her fingers slippy with blood
she'll clumsy a tool and drop it – then
he'll slap another into her palm

under the white masks their eyes don't meet
they don't converse   raprap go their voices
purposeful intent in the quiet room

If you commit yourself here the man's voice says
(Oh she is committed) *we might make a baby
and it might be fine and it might be dead*

something sharp and steely clatters from her hand
the neighbour's baby displayed on the sideboard
the narrow nasty yellow box women-whispers

she remembers stains on the cottonwool
plugging its nostrils   the candle face
above a white frilled cover

where she comes from you must touch
the dead – she tells him of the fist
her fingers made refusing

now she holds out her hand flat
as though for caning   this time
he gentles the knife into it

Finality of Egg

whitecoated syllables in a hot quiet room
head listening, not hearing air become words
     sorry   *a miracle*   *adoption*   *…to terms*
she hears somebody crying saying   Oh no No

centuries later hearing her feet scrunch
through shingle not looking back   caught
eyes squint not to see the lozenge lights
off sunburnt sea no eyes air where mind was

home in a greenshade kitchen clockwork hands
shred chop slice whisk mix – can't not marvel
at hand design there in this caught minute
till aeons later the darkhaired man comes

flowers card a greenglass bottle of wine –
she had forgotten that other moment – two kids
in their twenties a plaster cake words loud
in a still silence her body weeps for what is lost

she has no body – a stone on a beach – she has
no eyes – seaglare has blinded she has no voice –
it can't be her voice saying *miracle adoption sorry*
while eggs surface bluely through white mayonnaise

Theatre

Two glass circles in the door. No real
windows. The room is all hard light.
On the steel table a woman is lying
flat on her back with closed eyes.

A man is feeding her air.
Another man is making a slit in her skin
parting the fat and muscle
just below her belly's swell.

His hands are the colour of corpse
in surgical gloves but quick and deft.
He is reaching into her body.
He is removing a part of her.

Now he is sewing up the flesh
with small neat stitches –
snapsnap go the scissors
as the thread's snipped off.

There are seventeen black stitches
like a line of barbed wire
just above the pubic bone, behind them
a pear shaped pocket of air.

The woman sees none of this.
Her recording mind is whirring
useless in a deep black gap.
It will be someone else's memory.

Hers is waking in another room
wrapped from neck to toe in tinfoil
and the dark-haired man's joke
about a chicken ready for roasting.

She remembers the wobble in his laugh
and the way his eyes try to meet hers,
almost succeed, till lozenges of reflected
silver foil get in the way.

Cuckoo Calling

If she could feel, spring would appal
the world running its egg-and-sperm race
the birdcall blatant with demand.

She is stone: black; heavy; inert.
Where flesh was, moss grows.
Where hope was there is a gap.

In the gap the cuckoo came calling
a flap of wing among trees
and fast and unseen filled it.

At the Garden Centre

The garden-centre son is a bird man,
foster-father to falcons he's reared
from eggs to chicks to adult birds.

I watched him build the nesting-box
with large sure hands, drive nails true,
cut and sand the entrance to smooth.

I've watched him fix it above the tank,
watched the starlings reconnoitre,
enter and re-enter with strings of grass.

Now there are eggs; four eggs; pale blue
freckled brown. He and I are counting days.
10, 11, 12 – soon there will be nestlings.

Christ! What is he doing, the man? Why
does he enter his hand in the entrance hole
in the starling's absence, palm and heft her eggs?

My mind flaps with questions. Someone else
tells me, for the man sidesteps my eyes.
He is fingertipping for imminent fracture –

when the triangular gap breaches the shell
when slimed baldiness of fledgling dints
his finger, he'll feed them to his falcons.

Separating Eggs

Nan's practised fingers preparing meringue
– quick one-two-three flick of her hand –
two perfect shell-halves arced into the bin.

Do I remember, or was it a story, one about
a bad girl who threw shells on the fire,
stupid girl who stopped all the hens laying?

Ma's stainless steel fingers slicing toast soldiers
guillotining the head off the egg with a buttery knife.
A bad girl with a mouth compressed to a line –

a naughty bad child who'll never grow big with furious
tears at the soldiers' forced entry, yolk on her chin.
Or is it a story?

There are hags in my kitchen – crowds of them
with similar features. They're laughing over some task
in common – weaving or cooking – I can't make it out.

Their disembodied voices are snarling my fingers up,
clumsying the tips so I can't get the cut clean enough,
the crack sharp enough, the timing spot-on.

Till I get it right, my soufflés will never rise.

Gifts

I am no lover of chocolate.
Savour and spice mean more to me
than sweet. They know it.

For Easter they have given me
a Chinese painted egg, ten open
anemones and a homemade card.

I assault the grain of their cheeks
with great smacking kisses till they smile
their pinkest smiles. I smile too,

savouring the notion of cuckoos
offering gifts of egg to repay
and say thank you.

Oh, it's cupboard love (they know somewhere
I have chocolate eggs for them) but
as cupboard lovers they are truly authentic,

big grabbing greedy beautiful chicks.
Look at their light blue eyes, pale skin,
straight fall of hair –

it's passing strange how they resemble me,
except they're chocolate-lovers.

Lemon Soufflé Omelette

This is a light, foamy, lemony pudding, literally made in moments.
                             Delia Smith's Cookery Course Part 1

There are just the two of them.
The woman has separated her eggs.
Now she is adding bitter and sharp,
now sweet. Now she is whisking them.
Now she is cooking them, folding
and stirring to prevent them sticking.

Look at her face as she carries the dish to the table,
the lighted brandy playing its blues on the surface
of what she's produced. Is it appetite, or pride
or simple pleasure that turns her mouth up so in its U?
Or is it that it took so few moments to make
and will serve two people?

Thinking Egg

In the warm kitchen
two women are sitting
confiding failings, fears.
One woman is me.

..... like an egg I'm saying
one minute tough enough
to withstand anything, next
a fingertip could crack me...

The other woman is literal –
she'll have no truck with metaphor
No   she's saying   No you are not
an egg   You are a woman

and yes, my literal friend,
I guess you are right,
but I'm a woman thinking egg
and staggering under its weight.

JACQUELINE BROWN was born in Pontefract, West Yorkshire in 1944, and was educated there and at the University of Newcastle-upon-Tyne, where she gained a B.A. in French and English. It was a course run by the poet U.A. Fanthorpe at the Arvon Foundation that started her off on her own writing career, although it is only now, some eight years later, that she feels able to describe herself as a poet.

Her work has appeared in a wide variety of magazines and journals including *The Observer*, *Poetry Review* and *Staple*, and her first collection of poems, *Accidental Reality* was published by Littlewood in 1989. In 1992, she had the distinction of winning the first prize in the Observer/Arvon Poetry Competition with the then unpublished sequence of poems *Thinking Egg*.

Having taught for many years both in this country and abroad, Jacqueline Brown currently teaches creative writing at the W.E.A. and also to adults and children with mental health problems. She lives with her husband and two adopted daughters in Derbyshire.